The Impressionists

Vanessa Whinney

ATHENA
INTERNATIONAL

The Impressionists

Introduction

Impressionism is enormously popular as an art movement, even one hundred or so years after its heyday. This is almost unique in the history of art where so often the taste for artistic styles and eras fluctuates according to fashion. No other group of artists' pictures are so widely known to people of all social levels, nor so loved. Their popularity has many causes. One major factor is the brightness, gaiety and joy with which they are infused. We can view them as Old Masters enshrined on the walls of museums. And because of the proliferation of low-cost reproductions, we can enjoy them even in the living-rooms of our own homes. In the 1860s and 70s, when Monet and his circle were launching their revolutionary canvases on a startled public, it was a very different story. Then there was certainly no universal acceptance.

It is interesting to delve briefly into the background influences on the Impressionists. We can trace hints of an Impressionist style in many of their artistic predecessors, some of whom such as Delacroix were still alive when they were studying. Of particular interest are the indirect influences of new technological and mechanical discoveries, such as photography. Photography affected them in several ways. Firstly it made painting superfluous as a record of important national and historical events. The camera was far more instantaneous and effective as a reporter than a labour of many months with oil and canvas could ever be. In a subtle and gradual way, the rôle of the artist began to change. He could no longer rely on large official commissions from the state or monarch; painting began to be chiefly a means of decoration or social comment, a more personal statement by the artist.

All this did not happen overnight, but these developments took on a new dimension with the art of the Impressionists, and laid the foundations for modern art. In a less obvious way, photography influenced the composition of their pictures. The eye of the camera often distorts the picture, for instance, enlarging the foreground area, or cutting off figures or objects arbitrarily, a device which Degas used in his paintings to great effect. It is noteworthy that early experiments in cinematic photography, begun in 1872 by Eadweard Muybridge, revealed for the first time the way an animal's legs move in motion. Degas among others was quick to utilize this discovery in his race-course paintings, where the galloping steeds move naturally, without the artificial, suspended effect of moving horses in great paintings of the past.

In the field of painting, early manifestations of Impressionism can be traced in the work of the English artists Constable and Turner. In the first half of the nineteenth century, Constable was painting landscapes based on his on-the-spot sketches and cloud studies. Turner often painted for his own pleasure, as well as taking commissions, and his explosions of golden light are very 'impressionist'. These two painters had an indirect influence on at least Monet and Pissarro, who visited London in 1870 and had an opportunity of seeing the national collections there; and Sisley, who was the son of an emigré Englishman, spent his youth studying in England before taking up art seriously.

In France, a gathering of rural painters called the Barbizon group painted in the primeval forest of Fontainebleau, making sketches in the open, but generally finishing them in the studio. Nearly thirty years later, in 1864, Monet and his friends followed in their footsteps, but they started and finished out in the open. Monet as an individual had early contact with Boudin, who owned a framer's shop in Le Havre where Monet was born. Boudin saw Monet's early caricatures in 1858 and persuaded him to paint in oils on the shore, as Boudin himself did. Monet also met the Dutchman Jongkind who used a very light palette and encouraged Monet to do the same. Pissarro found inspiration in Corot's paintings, which he first saw at the Universal Exhibition in Paris in 1855. Corot was associated with the Barbizon group, and was instrumental in Pissarro's becoming a lifelong devotee to *plein-air* (open air) painting. For many years Pissarro even styled himself 'pupil of Corot' when exhibiting, and his early work is very close in style to Corot (see page 34). Courbet, another Barbizon associate, had a stand at the 1865 Universal Exhibition, and was a regular contributor to the Salon. Courbet was one of the first artists to paint ordinary people enjoying the delights of life, a theme basic to Impressionism. One of his pictures of two girls on the banks of the Seine caused quite a stir at the Salon of 1857, since they were obviously portraits of well-known women of whom one was dressed only in her petticoats!

The Salon played a very important rôle in the artistic life of nineteenth century Paris. It was virtually the only place where paintings could be seen by critics, connoisseurs and, most important of all, buyers. Every two years (and after 1863, every year) artists would submit their work, and a selection for exhibition was made by a jury. Academic subjects and conservative methods were favoured, so that if new ideas and styles were accepted, they could arouse quite hostile emotions in the viewers. But more often than not, they were not accepted, as happened with a vengeance in 1863, when the jury rejected three-fifths of the submitted works. There was such an outcry that the Emperor Napoleon III ordered the 'refused' works to be exhibited at what became known as the *Salon des Refusés*. Included were paintings by Manet, Pissarro, Cézanne, Jongkind and Whistler, amongst many others.

Manet: Le Déjeuner Sur L'Herbe (detail).

The principal attraction was Manet's **Le Déjeuner sur l'Herbe**, which caused a national scandal because of its daring inclusion of a naked woman seated in a forest in the company of two fully clothed men (see above and pages 28-29).

The *Salon des Refusés* provided exposure to the public eye, but it was a far from ideal situation. First, there was fierce criticism and ridicule (although there were a few sympathetic voices); second, the stigma of having been 'refused' was rather negative. A group show of their own was discussed as early as 1867 by Monet and Bazille, but a number of important developments took place before the first Impressionist exhibition.

Most of the group knew each other by the early 1860s. Monet and Pissarro first met in 1850 at the Académie Suisse, an art-teaching establishment in Paris. In 1861, Cézanne joined them, and he was to study there on and off for the next four years, since he was unable to pass the entrance examinations to the Ecole des Beaux Arts where other members of the group studied. Monet graduated to the Ecole des Beaux Arts in

1862, under the tutelage of Gleyre. There he worked with Renoir, Sisley and Bazille. The value of that period lay in the contact with other artists rather than in Gleyre's teaching, which was in any case largely *laissez-faire*; and what there was of it was very academic. He would insist that they draw nudes with an eye on the antique, idealising everything, instead of conveying the character of the model. He also strongly disapproved of the use of bright colours, as used by Renoir, for example.

On the closure of Gleyre's studio in 1864, Monet, Renoir, Sisley and Bazille worked together in Chailly near Barbizon, painting Fontainebleau forest in the open air. From then on, there was constant contact, not only between these four, but also with Pissarro, Manet, Degas and Cézanne. Manet gathered around him a circle of contemporary artists and writers for discussions at the Café Guerbois in Paris, usually on Thursday evenings, but often at other times too. The discussions were very animated and stimulating, on political as well as artistic subjects. Later, in about 1876, they transferred their affections to the Café de la Nouvelle-Athènes, and its leading light, the Bohemian artist Desboutin, was immortalised, with the actress Ellen Andrée, in Degas' painting **L'Absinthe** (see right and page 43).

One of the most discussed subjects was the newly discovered Japanese print. Since they were first exhibited in 1862, these prints were widely circulated in the city, and wrought far-reaching transformations on the work of many artists of differing ages and persuasions. Whistler dressed his models in Japanese costumes. Manet painted a portrait of Zola in about 1867 (now in the Louvre) with a Japanese screen behind him and a Japanese print on the wall. He also adapted the flat linear style of these prints for his own purposes, as for instance in **The Fifer** (see page 30). Monet painted his wife in a highly decorated Japanese costume against a background of oriental fans in 1876 (now in the Boston Museum of Fine Arts). Degas was particularly impressed by the foreshortening effects, off-centre composition and high viewpoint characteristic of the prints. When in the 1880s van Gogh encountered them, he was so inspired that he felt he was going to Japan itself when he went south to Arles (see page 56). He too adapted the themes and style of the prints to his own peculiar vision of the world, and painted a loving portrait of Père Tanguy with a background consisting entirely of oriental prints (now in the Musée Rodin, Paris).

In 1869, Renoir and Monet worked together at La Grenouillère, a café on the banks of the Seine. Their extreme poverty meant that they often could not afford even to buy paints. They evolved the Impressionist technique of painting with rapid brushstrokes and dabs of colour. They shunned the use of black or brown, and achieved tones, lights and darks, by juxtaposing pure colour. This was particularly effective when painting water, and conveyed its shimmering reflective surface ideally. The method was a natural result of their out-of-doors work over the previous few years, but on this occasion they worked closer together than at any other time, even painting the same subjects.

On 18th July 1870, the Franco-Prussian war broke out, resulting in disruption to normal daily life. Manet, Degas, Renoir and Bazille all enlisted and served in the French army. Bazille was tragically killed in November, thus depriving the world of one of the group's most promising talents. Monet and Pissarro both removed to

Degas: L'Absinthe (detail).

England to avoid being drafted, since their political views opposed the idea of service in the Emperor's army. The encounter between these two in London in 1870 was very beneficial, particularly for Pissarro, who learnt much from Monet about his technique of painting in the open air. They made an important contact in the person of Durand-Ruel, the art dealer, who was attempting to interest British buyers in the works of the Barbizon school. From then on, together with Ambroise Vollard, he became the Impressionists' most faithful dealer. The British were not sympathetic to Monet's new ideas, and the two artists were glad to return home after the Paris *Commune* – a period of political anarchy during the months of March to May 1871.

Many of the group had suffered personal setbacks. Apart from the tragedy of Bazille, all Pissarro's paintings, left at his home in Louveciennes, were destroyed. Sisley's father, a prosperous merchant, was bankrupted by the war and died soon after, leaving his son without support. A new era began, and although optimism may at first have been high, security and prosperity were still a long way off.

Manet: Monet's Boat (detail).

There was another *Salon des Refusés* in 1873, which was as unsatisfactory to the participants as the first one had been. They decided to launch their own group show. This opened on 15 April 1874 in the premises of the photographer Nadar. All but Manet were represented, along with at least twenty others. Manet refused to show with them, preferring to be represented in the official Salon when accepted. The group were not then known by the name Impressionists; instead they exhibited under the title 'Société anonyme des artistes peintres, sculpt-

eurs, graveurs, etc.' They came to be called 'Impressionists' as a result of an article by the critic Louis Leroy in the paper *Charivari*. He called his article 'Exhibition of the Impressionists', the idea for which undoubtedly came from the title of Monet's picture **Impression: Sunrise**, a misty morning view of Le Havre harbour (see pages 24-25). The article was derisory in tone, but the name has stuck.

The results of the exhibition were disappointing. Financially it was a disaster, as the income was insufficient to pay their debts. The lack of interest from the general public was most discouraging, and the prospects for the indigent among them very bleak. Nevertheless, nearly all the friends were able to paint together at Argenteuil in the summer of 1874, where Monet acquired a floating studio. He got the idea from Daubigny, who had had a boat on the river Oise in 1857 from which to paint. Manet has left a charming record of Monet and his wife on their boat (see left and page 31). For the first time, Manet had come to work alongside Monet, who impressed him enormously. Manet's Argenteuil period is his most Impressionist, and strikingly different from his earlier style. He painted out-of-doors, adopted a lighter, more brightly coloured palette and used smaller brushstrokes. Owing to the lack of sales from the first group exhibition, and desperate to make a living from his painting, Renoir persuaded his companions to join him in holding an auction sale of their work. This took place in March 1875, but proved to be yet another serious setback, as the bids failed even to cover the cost of materials and frames. The only good thing to come out of the auction was the appearance of Victor Chocquet. A customs official of modest means, he attended the sale but bought nothing. He noticed and liked Renoir's paintings, and afterwards approached the artist to request him to paint his wife. He compared Renoir to Delacroix, some of whose paintings he owned, and of course, the flattered Renoir was delighted to accept. Renoir introduced him to Cézanne, and Chocquet thereafter became a faithful patron of them both, and to a lesser degree of Monet. Chocquet was tireless in his support of his new friends, and during the second Impressionist exhibition in 1876 spent much time trying to persuade members of the public to share his enthusiasm – but largely without success. Albert Wolff, the art critic, wrote a vindictive diatribe about that show in his newspaper *Le Figaro*. It so incensed Eugène Manet, the painter's brother, that he had to be dissuaded from challenging Wolff to a duel!

The years 1876–77 saw the creation of some of the greatest Impressionist masterpieces. Works such as Sisley's **Floods at Port Marley** (page 39), Renoir's **Le Moulin de la Galette** (pages 12-13), Monet's **Gare Saint-Lazare** (page 26), Pissarro's **Red Roofs** (pages 36-37) and Degas' **L'Absinthe** (pages 7 and 43) all date from this period. At the same time, they were beginning to be known outside France, in particular in the United States, partly through the efforts of the American artist Mary Cassatt, who met Degas in 1877, and who subsequently exhibited with the group.

There were six more group exhibitions, making eight in all, but not all the original members participated in each of them. Manet never showed with them. Pissarro was involved in all of them. The others fluctuated in their fidelity. As their reputation grew, they were joined by other artists. Of the younger generation, the most interesting newcomers were Paul Gauguin, who first joined at the invitation of Pissarro and Degas in 1879 for the fourth show; and Seurat, who exhibited in the last show in 1886. These two were admitted, but not without some opposition. Monet was impatient at the influx of 'dabblers' who regarded themselves as Impressionists – a criticism quite likely levelled at Gauguin, who was in effect a 'Sunday painter' until 1882, though of course his work was far from amateur. Seurat was objected to because his *pointillist* method was considered anti-Impressionist, though it certainly stemmed from it.

By the 1880s the artists were mostly following independent courses, and Monet even went so far as to say on one occasion that he preferred not to work with Renoir – a strange contrast to the Argenteuil days. Some of them, in particular Renoir, became dissatisfied with Impressionism, and sought new channels of inspiration. Only Sisley remained totally faithful to the original concept. Even Pissarro investigated Seurat's *pointillism* for a number of years. Manet, who died in 1883, explored *genre* subjects towards the end, as in **The Bar at the Folies-Bergère** (page 33). Degas turned to studies of women active in their daily work, such as laundresses and milliners, and also to subtle and delicate pastel drawings of nudes bathing or at their *toilette* (pages 44-45). Monet experimented with several canvases of roughly the same size, painting the same scene on each one in turn, replacing the canvas when the light or atmospheric conditions changed. He completed several series in this vein. Fifteen paintings of **Haystacks** were exhibited at Durand-Ruel's in 1891. Monet initially thought two canvases would be enough to convey the different moods, but in practice found he needed many more to capture the continuously changing light. These, and his other series on **Rouen Cathedral Façade, Poplars, Waterlilies** in his pond at Giverny and views of London, were all very popular and sold well.

Success, it seemed, had finally arrived. It was too late for some, like Manet and Sisley, whose works only soared in value after their deaths. But Monet and Renoir in particular began to reap the benefits of belated public recognition. In 1886, the same year as the last Impressionist exhibition, Durand-Ruel organised a successful show in New York of three hundred canvases, including works by Degas, Pissarro, Monet, Manet, Renoir, Sisley and Seurat. It was also in 1886 that Vincent van Gogh came to Paris to stay with his brother Theo, and was overwhelmed with admiration for the Impressionists. He of course evolved his own style, as did all the Post-Impressionists, and this pained Pissarro, to whom van Gogh, Gauguin and Seurat all owed a debt of gratitude for his early sponsorship and recognition of their talent. But the time had come for the branches to grow out from the parent plant, and for the seedlings to multiply and manifest themselves in the many subsequent art movements that sprang from Impressionism.

Path Climbing Through Long Grass. 1874. Oil on canvas, 59 x 74cm. Louvre, Paris.

During the period 1872 to 1878, Renoir, Monet, Sisley and Manet frequently worked together at the village of Argenteuil on the outskirts of Paris. Monet's influence was far-reaching, and he persuaded them all to paint in the open air. He and Renoir had also worked together in 1869 and painted the same subjects.
When Path Climbing Through Long Grass *is compared*

with Monet's Field with Poppies *(page 26), we can see the similarity of subject and composition. Whereas Monet eventually abandoned figure painting for pure landscape, Renoir could never resist the human touch. The brilliant red of the sunshade provides an excellent focal point, which, together with the scattering of red flowers in the foreground, lightens the predominant lush green of a midsummer scene.*

AUGUSTE RENOIR 1841–1919

Renoir is the artist whom one perhaps thinks of first when the Impressionists are mentioned. His art is the most accessible to the man in the street, with its optimism and pleasure in the senses. The brilliant colours and soft technique, the children, and above all the beautiful women, are the trademarks of his painting which everyone knows.

His artistic ability emerged at an early age, so his parents apprenticed him to a porcelain painting factory. When that went out of business, he painted fans, basing his designs on works by Watteau, Fragonard and Boucher which he saw and copied in the Louvre.

In 1862 he entered the studio of Gleyre in Paris, where he studied along with Monet, Sisley and Bazille. The friendships formed were of far greater significance than the ideas of Gleyre, which were the opposite of his own. On being told 'one does not paint for amusement', Renoir replied 'If it didn't amuse me, I shouldn't paint' – which sums up his whole attitude. All his life his purpose was to paint for the joy of it.

His early work shows the influence of Manet, whose **Le Déjeuner sur l'Herbe** of 1863 (pages 28-29) aroused enormous controversy in the *Salon des Refusés* of that year. In 1869 he and Monet worked side by side at La Grenouillère, a riverside restaurant on the Seine, and evolved the technique of applying pure unmixed colours (not black or brown) with small brushstrokes to give an 'impression' of a scene. The artists were very poor. Once Renoir filled his pockets with bread from his parents' table to give Monet, who was literally starving.

The Franco-Prussian war of 1870 was a difficult period for everyone, and in the confusion and economic depression which followed the plight of these artists was more desperate than ever. In the year of the first Impressionist exhibition, 1874, public ridicule was poured on their work, even though some of the finest Impressionist paintings were shown. The next year, following an auction of Impressionist works, Renoir's fortunes changed. He found a patron in the person of Victor Chocquet, a customs official of modest means, but with excellent taste, who had a small collection of Delacroix paintings, and who from then on regularly bought and commissioned paintings from him and some of his colleagues, in particular Cézanne. He also met the publisher Georges Charpentier, and through his patronage came to be regarded as a fashionable society painter, especially of children. He was at last able to rise above the grinding hardships of poverty and take stock of his development, and even travel abroad. He was particularly impressed, on a visit to Italy, by the works of Raphael, and by the Pompeii frescoes.

This broadening of his experience resulted in a dissatisfaction with Impressionism and with his own technique, which he felt lacked the basis of good draughtsmanship. He therefore adopted a linear style which is known as his 'dry' period, and is discernible in parts of **Les Parapluies** (page 19). Although he did not persist in this style for very long, he never really returned to his early manner. His marriage gave him an opportunity to paint maternal subjects. This produced a less brittle effect, and he began to use the hot colours which are so characteristic of his late work.

His last years were overshadowed by an arthritic condition which eventually confined him to a wheelchair. But amazingly, he outlived all his fellow Impressionists except Monet, painting to the end with a brush taped to his hand, and he did not die until 1919.

Renoir

Renoir was intrigued by the local people who came every Sunday to the open-air café depicted here, to dance and meet friends. The name Le Moulin de la Galette is derived from a windmill then on the site. Renoir rented rooms nearby, and every day his canvas was carried by friends to the café so that he could paint outdoors. Before this time, painters might have sketched such a scene as this outside; but the final painting would have been finished in the studio, with the models posing there. Thus they would often appear incongruous and stiff. Although Renoir undoubtedly did make some finishing touches in the studio, the main work was painted on the spot, as can be seen from the dappled light which filters through the trees onto the figures and from the happy air of casual informality, effects which would have been impossible to duplicate in the studio.

Several of Renoir's friends posed for him: in the foreground with a striped dress is Estelle, the sister of Renoir's model Jeanne; another model, Margot, is dancing with a Cuban painter (see detail). There is another group of his friends around the table on the right.

Unfortunately, as Renoir himself acknowledged in his last years, the colours have changed since he painted it, giving the work a predominantly blue tone which it did not have originally.

Le Moulin de la Galette, 1876. Oil on canvas, 131 x 175cm. Louvre, Paris.

The pigments in The Swing *have discoloured over the years, giving it the same blue tinge as* Le Moulin de la Galette *(page 12). The two pictures were painted in the same year – in fact at the same time, for Renoir worked on this painting in the morning in the garden of his home at 78 rue Cortot, and on* Le Moulin *in the afternoon.*

As usual Renoir used his friends as models, with his favourite, Jeanne, clutching the ropes of a swing. The actual and visual instability, suggested by the swing and Jeanne's almost floating female form, is balanced by the stability of the man with his back to us, who has his feet firmly on the ground.

The Swing, 1876. Oil on canvas, 92 x 73cm. Louvre, Paris.

As subjects for paintings, women dominated Renoir's life. He conveyed their femininity and soft rounded forms with unequalled mastery. Little girls were no less lovingly treated. Sometimes they were onlookers in large canvases, as for instance in Les Parapluies (page 19); at other times, as here, they played a unique role. They were immensely appealling, stealing the limelight, but real children, not miniature adults.

It was his gift for painting children which enabled Renoir to establish his career as a society portrait painter in the late 1870's and to overcome his major economic difficulties.

Renoir rarely missed the opportunity to add a splash of bright colour – note the brilliant red ribbon in the child's hair. He used the same device in Path Climbing Through Long Grass (Page 10).

A Girl with a Watering Can, 1876. Oil on canvas, 100.3 x 73.2cm. National Gallery of Art, Washington, Chester Dale Collection.

This painting and Le Moulin de la Galette *are Renoir's supreme masterpieces depicting ordinary people – indeed personal friends of the artist – enjoying themselves in their leisure time. The composition of the* Luncheon *is unified and complete – and yet the painting is full of delightful individual details, such as the provocative pout of the pretty girl on the left (Aline Charigot whom Renoir married in 1890), playing with her little terrier; the 'still life' of fruit and drink on the table, indicating the disarray characteristic of a meal enjoyed and now finished; the tantalizing vignette of the river seen through the awning on the left; the flirtatious blonde on the right with her two admirers; and the seductive pose of the girl leaning on the balustrade (see detail). One can imagine a happy band of young undergraduates today after a morning's punting enjoying just such a luncheon.*

This is Renoir's last major work in the Impressionist style of his early years, as soon afterwards he realised the need for more substance in his figures. Indeed, the boatman on the right, and especially his muscular arm, has a more solid look about him than comparable figures in Le Moulin de la Galette.

Luncheon of the Boating Party, 1881. Oil on canvas, 130 x 173cm. Phillips Collection, Washington.

Left: **Dance at Bougival,** 1883. Oil on canvas, 179 x 98cm. Museum of Fine Arts, Boston.

This is one of a series of dancing couples in much the same setting as Le Moulin de la Galette – *dancing out of doors with drinkers nearby at a café table. But here the dancers have more prominence. Renoir's love of the lyrical and graceful surfaced continually in such paintings, and dancers occurred frequently in his work throughout his life. He rarely painted ballet dancers in the manner of Degas (with the exception of one shimmering ballerina which is in Washington) – usually peasant or folk dancers, full of movement.*

Les Parapluies, *c.*1884. Oil on canvas, 180 x 115cm. National Gallery, London.

Les Parapluies, *or* The Umbrellas, *is an example of Renoir's renewed attention to composition, for the umbrellas form a balanced pattern in the background. The picture in particular illustrates the transitional aspect of his work, when he was seeking a firmer, more linear basis in place of Impressionism. It is almost certain that extensive re-working took place, which would explain the difference between the two discernible styles. The little girls in the front, and the woman looking down on them, are in his earlier style, whereas the woman with the band-box, and most of the rest of the picture, were painted later.*
The child with the hoop (see detail) is one of Renoir's most appealing creations. She demonstrates his genius for painting children to look like children, and not like miniature adults, as they had so often been depicted in the past.

After a period of reaction against Impressionism, and the adoption of a dry technique, Renoir's painting gradually softened again, and his late work is often referred to as his 'red' period because of the hotter colours he used. La Dormeuse, or The Sleeper, is 'cooler' than many he painted towards the end of his life, but the myriad colours of pink, yellow, purple are there in the flesh tones – giving an impression of skin colour. He frequently used the theme of a sensuous draped bather in his later years, and Gabrielle the family maid often posed for him.

La Dormeuse, 1897. Oil on canvas, 81 x 65.5cm. Oskar Reinhart Collection, Winterthur.

CLAUDE MONET 1840–1926

The career of Monet was not only the longest of the group (he did not die until 1926), but he was also the most truly Impressionist painter of them all.

He came from a working class family, who early on encouraged his talent, but later, becoming suspicious of his revolutionary artistic ideas and bohemian way of life, abandoned him to his fate. His earliest works consisted of caricatures. In Le Havre, however, where he was brought up, he met Boudin, who encouraged him to paint in the open air. His lifelong interest in the sea, and water in .general, no doubt stems from his familiarity with and love of Le Havre.

In 1859 he visited Paris and studied at the Académie Suisse, where he first met Pissarro. Later, in 1862, he entered the studio of Gleyre and met Renoir, Sisley and Bazille.

After the stir caused by Manet's **Le Déjeuner sur l'Herbe** in 1863, Monet embarked on several large-scale paintings dominated by figures and painted in the open air, such as **Women in the Garden.** To paint such large canvases outside caused him considerable practical difficulties, and also financial embarrassment because of their cost. For most of his life he was incredibly poor. He became extremely bitter over this, so much so that he even expressed aggressive ingratitude to some of those who tried to help him, in particular his friend Bazille. His family had cut off his allowance, and his mistress, Camille, was bearing him children. Often he could not afford to buy food, let alone paints and canvas. Yet his work was making great strides, and in 1869 he and Renoir discovered the Impressionist technique of dividing the paint into dabs of pure colour to obtain the effect or 'impression' of an object or a view.

1870 was an eventful year, for in June he married Camille, and in July the Franco-Prussian war broke out. Monet, being anti-Royalist, did not wish to enlist to fight for Napoleon III, so he fled to England. There he found Pissarro, and also met Durand-Ruel, who became the Impressionists' most loyal dealer. There too he may have been influenced by Turner and Constable, though by this time his own course was already set. The two Impressionists were not appreciated by the London art world, and were glad to return to France, but Monet never forgot the enticing mists and fog of London, which he returned to paint many years later in a most memorable series (see page 27).

The first Impressionist exhibition was held in 1874; most of the paintings were held up to public ridicule, in particular his picture **Impression: Sunrise**, which gave the group its name (pages 24–25).

Monet painted several series: **Gare Saint-Lazare** in 1876 (page 26) and **Haystacks, Poplars on the Epte,** and **Rouen Cathedral** in the 1890s. He evolved the idea of painting on several canvases at the same time, and for the purpose he had a special slotted box which contained the canvases – all roughly the same size – so that he could choose the one most suitable for the light of the moment. In 1900 he embarked on his Thames series, and also started a series of water-lily paintings which he elaborated to the end of his life. He had by now received belated public recognition (following a successful exhibition with the sculptor Rodin in 1889), and was able to settle at Giverny. He created a water lily pond there with a bridge; this became the subject of his last great work, commissioned by the French state. It was a semi-abstract explosion of colour and light on an enormous scale which occupied him for ten years.

Women in the Garden, 1866–67. Oil on canvas, 255 x 205cm. Louvre, Paris.

Terrace at Sainte-Adresse, *c.*1866. Oil on canvas, 97.8 x 132cm. Metropolitan Museum of Art, New York.

This picture and Woman in the Garden *were painted at the same period and show obvious stylistic similarities. The people in the garden at Sainte-Adresse are traditionally identified as members of Monet's family. You can almost feel the breezes blowing in from the sea on the hot, clear August morning – the month is identifiable from the gladioli in bloom. In the distance is probably Le Havre, often painted by Monet, and sketched again five years later with historic results for him and his fellow artists (see page* 25 *).*

Women in the Garden *was painted in the garden of the house Monet rented at Ville d'Avray, and because of its huge size the canvas had to be lowered into a specially dug trench so that he could reach the upper parts. This greatly amused the artist Courbet on his visits to the young Monet.*
It is said that the picture was suggested by Bazille, who had painted a conversation piece of his family outside in a garden. The people in Monet's picture are thought to be also of Bazille's family, but painted from photographs, with Monet's mistress Camille posing for each figure in turn. As Monet was permanently in debt, and as the picture could not sell at the Salon because it was refused, Bazille bought it himself for 2,500 *francs which he paid in monthly instalments. Yet despite Monet's personal hardships, he was able to suffuse this masterpiece with lightness and gaiety.*

It was through this painting that the name 'Impressionists' came to be given to the group in 1874. In order to defy the official Salon, from whose walls their pictures had been effectively banned, they held their first exhibition that year on the photographer Nadar's premises. The art critic Leroy wrote an article about the exhibition and made disparaging remarks about this and other paintings, and called the group 'Impressionists' in the title to his article. It was intended as an insult, but the name has remained.

Although the painting is just a sketch, it is obviously very carefully composed. The view is of Le Havre harbour seen through early morning mist. It is an industrial scene, yet the clear limpid stillness remainds one of a country lake. If viewed through half-closed eyes or from a great distance, the three boats in the foreground become clear and in focus, and the whole has great depth. It is very delicate, jewel-like and fresh, with its pastel pinks and grey-blues – rather a romanticised view; but the careful observations and brilliant rendering of light and reflections confirm this as a masterpiece.

Impression: Sunrise, 1872. Oil on canvas, 50 x 62cm. Marmottan Museum, Paris.

Left: **A Field with Poppies,** 1873. Oil on canvas, 49.5 x 64.7cm. Louvre, Paris.

From the 1870's Monet concentrated mainly on landscapes and nature in all her moods. The figures here are less prominent, and in his subsequent work played a lessening role. Compare this with Renoir's Path Climbing Through Long Grass *(page 10), painted when the two artists were working together. Monet revels in the richness and abundance of colour in the mass of red poppies. The meadow to the right is not green but has that subtle purplish tinge characteristic of the heads of grasses when their seeds are ready to blow away in the breeze. What accurate observation of a midsummer moment!*

Monet first explored the varied effects light could have on a given subject with the Gare Saint-Lazare series. He painted at least four canvases from this spot, looking out at the trains from under the shed. Another six or so were painted at the station in different locations. He was especially interested in the effect of steam, in the same way as he was captivated by London fog. Perhaps he was influenced by Turner's Rain, Steam and Speed, which he would have seen in London.
Later, he used the series idea more scientifically. When painting Rouen Cathedral, for instance, he would work on several canvases of similar size, kept in a slotted box, changing the canvases when the light altered.

Left: **Gare Saint-Lazare,** 1877. Oil on canvas, 75 x 100cm. Louvre, Paris.

Houses of Parliament, 1904. Oil on canvas, 81.3 x 91.4cm. Louvre, Paris.

In 1870 Monet had fled to England to avoid involvement in the Franco-Prussian war. The mists and fog of London fascinated him, and in later years he returned regularly to the city for several winters, staying at the Savoy hotel. From there he had a view of the Thames and Westminster and painted the effect of light and fog on the river. Water, with its subtle changes of light and reflection, was a life-long inspiration, and his last great series was of the water-lily pond in his garden. In Houses of Parliament he has brilliantly captured the ephemeral effect of the golden sun glistening on the water's surface, with the towers of Westminster shimmering through the mists of purple and blue.

Le Déjeuner sur L'Herbe, 1863. Oil on canvas, 214 x 270cm. Louvre, Paris.

EDOUARD MANET 1832–1883

Manet's background and upbringing were rather different to the majority of his artistic contemporaries. He was a product of the *haute bourgeoisie*, son of a magistrate, and he never had the struggle to support himself that Monet, Renoir and Pissarro suffered. He faithfully submitted his works to the official Salon, never exhibiting in the group shows of the Impressionists, even though he often had his works rejected. He preferred to try and change the traditions of the Salon by re-educating people through his *avant-garde* paintings, and to some extent he succeeded, though attracting hurtful abuse and criticism along the way. After the scandal over **Le Déjeuner sur L'Herbe** in 1863, he was regarded as a rebel, along with Monet and his circle. The group was even dubbed 'la bande à Manet', although Manet did not fully adopt an Impressionist style until 1874.

One of the main early influences on Manet was Spanish art and culture. He had an abiding love for Spain, which he visited in 1865, and was there able to study at first hand the works of Goya and Velasquez. Previously they had been known to him only from engravings. He frequently painted Spanish-looking women, such as Berthe Morisot, who married his brother Eugène. She would pose for him in Spanish costumes of black and white, colours he used extensively in the 1860's.

Like many of his contemporaries, he was inspired in a picture such as **The Fifer** (page 30) by the flat planes and linear composition of Japanese prints, then widely circulated. He incorporated prints and screens in the background of his portrait of Emile Zola of about 1867–8 (Louvre, Paris).

Besides posing for him, Berthe Morisot, who was an accomplished artist in her own right, encouraged Manet's step towards Impressionism and a closer association with Monet, Renoir and Bazille, all of whom regarded him as something of a hero for his stand against the Salon. He worked with Monet in the open air in 1874 at Argenteuil where he was impressed with the younger man's methods, to the extent that he brightened his own palette and adopted some of Monet's techniques. He never entirely abandoned his beloved black, but his late work shows the beneficial effect of the contact. He continued to make new discoveries right up to his tragic early death in 1883.

When Le Déjeuner (*or* Luncheon on the Grass) *was first exhibited in Paris in 1863 at the* Salon des Refusés *it caused a national scandal. One of the criticisms levelled against it was that it was a kind of parody of the great sixteenth century Venetian painter Giorgione's masterpiece* Concert Champêtre, *which still hangs in the Louvre. There the two nude females are classically draped, whereas Manet's nude had discarded her contemporary everyday dress in a heap on the grass. What was worse, she sat unashamedly naked in the presence of two Parisian gentlemen. And the Emperor thought the picture 'immodest'. Manet, who longed for acceptance, was now rejected by society. As a result he earned the respect and admiration of the young Impressionists, and found himself drawn, if rather reluctantly, into their circle.*

Le Déjeuner *might appear to have been painted in the open air, but in fact the figures were added in the studio. How apparent this is when compared with Renoir's later* Le Moulin de la Galette *(pages 12-13), which is infused with dappled light effects. Nevertheless, the strong broad planes of colour were far removed from the academic traditions of most of his contemporaries, and the forest surroundings are undoubtedly painted from life. There is great depth, partially achieved by means of the meandering stream which flows through the middle distance. The girl's clothes and the remains of their picnic form a delightful 'still life' in the bottom left of the picture.*

It is not hard to imagine how people felt in 1863 when they first beheld this picture; even now after over a hundred years, and conditioned by the permissive society, one feels a certain sense of shock when first confronted with it.

The Fifer, 1866. Oil on canvas, 164 x 97cm. Louvre, Paris.

This little boy has been described as 'surrounded by nothing but air', and was thought by the artist Daumier to resemble a playing card. In fact it is an example of Manet's concentration on the essentials – of clarity, harmony and economy. The brilliant red of his trousers is echoed in the cap, and the black side stripes form an outline emphasising the flat planes of colour. The subtle influence of the Japanese print is thus discreetly hinted at in the design. These prints were circulated in mid-nineteenth century Paris, and captured the imagination of many artists and connoisseurs.

Monet's Boat, 1874. Oil on canvas, 81 x 100cm. Neue Pinakothek, Munich.

Manet worked with Monet at Argenteuil during the summer of 1874. Monet had his floating studio there – a boat fitted out with a hut to house all his painting materials, and just enough space to sleep on in an emergency. He obtained the idea from the artist Daubigny, who was associated with the Barbizon group, and who was one of the earliest to work direct from nature. Daubigny had a small studio boat on the river Oise as early as 1857. The Argenteuil period was quite a momentous one in the history of Impressionism, because Renoir was also working with Monet, and they all three painted each other and made startling innovations in technique and style.

Here we have a charming document of a friend and fellow artist, with his wife, painting from the studio-boat. Monet needed friends, as he was permanently in debt, and Manet had to find him alternative accommodation when he was threatened with eviction from the boat for not paying the rent.

Manet's style changed dramatically, as can be seen by comparing the two pictures on these pages, when he started using small brushstrokes and bright colours in the Impressionist manner.

Only towards the end of his life did Manet begin to receive the recognition he longed for. This picture was not only accepted for the Salon of 1882, but also resulted in him being awarded the Légion d'Honneur. He had a genius for chronicling everyday life, and he drifted away from Monet's exploration of nature to concentrate on people.

Here is an extraordinary combination of portrait and still-life, and the main fascination lies in the fact that the entire area behind the girl is one huge mirror reflecting the whole scene before her. We see her own back view to the right and the gentlemen she is serving. Beyond is the audience waiting for the show to begin – or perhaps it is already under way, for there are some amusing touches, such as the feet of the trapeze artist just visible in the top left-hand corner. The lady with the opera glasses (see detail) focuses intently on something – whether the performance, or an admirer, we cannot tell. The barmaid herself, with a flower strategically placed on her décolleté, looks disinterested and far away, obviously bored by the routine of a place which provided fun and excitement for many.

Bar at the Folies-Bergère, 1881–2. Oil on canvas, 96 x 130cm. Courtauld Institute Galleries, London.

Varenne Saint-Hilaire, View from Champigny,
1863. Oil on canvas, 50 x 73cm. Museum of Fine Arts,
Budapest.

*This picture could almost be by Corot, it shows his influence so
markedly. It was painted in the year Pissarro's first child,
Lucien, was born, and the theme – peasants working in a field –
was one he frequently returned to throughout his life. He always
painted women and children with a sensitive touch, and being so
poor himself, obviously felt close to the country folk among
whom he lived.*

*This also shows the influence of Corot, who was an advocate of
plein air painting, and Pissarro remained faithful to this
method for most of his life. Pissarro's style changed considerably
in the latter part of 1870, for he left for France at the outbreak
of the Franco-Prussian war and worked with Monet in London,
where he absorbed many of Monet's Impressionist ideas.*

View from Louveciennes, *c*.1870. Oil on canvas,
52.7 x 82cm. National Gallery, London.

CAMILLE PISSARRO 1830–1903

Camille Pissarro was one of the most consistent practitioners of Impressionist technique, and a great influence on some of his contemporaries, especially the younger generation such as Cézanne, Van Gogh and Gauguin. He was born in 1830, which makes him the eldest of the group considered in this book.

His personal life was very turbulent, as he had an affair with his mother's maid, Julie Vellay, who bore him two children before they married in 1870, and seven in all. The eldest, Lucien, later became an accomplished painter in his own right. Pissarro suffered severe financial hardship for most of his life, but this is rarely reflected in his paintings, many of which are of sun-filled landscapes of the countryside he loved.

His early work (see left) was strongly influenced by Corot whom he met in 1855, and he even exhibited for a time as 'student of Corot'. His style developed noticeably in 1870, when he worked with Claude Monet in England, where they had both fled to avoid involvement in the Franco-Prussian war. He painted the effect of fog and snow and springtime – all of course executed in the open air. Monet's influence stimulated him, upon his return to France, to produce some of his finest work in the following years. In 1874 his work was included in the first Impressionist exhibition, and he showed pictures in all their subsequent exhibitions – indeed he was the most consistent supporter of the movement. In 1885 he experimented with the *pointillist* techniques of Seurat (see page 53) but did not find them altogether satisfactory, and abandoned them three years later.

In the last ten years of his life, his financial situation greatly improved, and his creative activity benefited. Despite a worsening eye infection, from 1897 to his death in 1903 he produced a series of views of Paris (see below), working from several different rented rooms. These paintings give a wonderful impression of the bustle of Parisian life at the turn of the century, and are among his greatest masterpieces.

Place du Théâtre Français, 1898. Oil on canvas, 72 x 93cm. County Museum of Art, Los Angeles.

In 1897 Pissarro embarked on a series of views of Paris, painted from windows of hotels and other buildings, since a problem with his eyes no longer made it comfortable for him to work in the open air. This view of the Place du Théâtre Français *was painted from the Hôtel du Louvre. The picture is interesting because it has no horizon, and Pissarro has captured the scene as a snapshot might – but with a painter's eye for colour and design.*

Red Roofs *is one of Pissarro's greatest paintings, done at a time when his contemporaries were also producing outstanding works. It is a good example of a pure Impressionist painting. Pissarro emphasized the importance of "placing tones everywhere with brush-strokes of the right colour and value" – and indeed, viewed close up (see detail), all one can see is a mosaic of brushstrokes. But looked at from a distance or through half-closed eyes, the picture comes into focus, and we can clearly distinguish the group of cottages and the different coloured fields in the distance. Despite his extreme poverty, it is a joyous picture, and vibrates with the glowing colours. The location is near his home in Pontoise, where he lived for twelve years from 1872-1884.*

Red Roofs, 1877. Oil on canvas, 53 x 64cm. Louvre, Paris.

ALFRED SISLEY 1839–1899

Sisley's parents were English, but he was born in Paris, and although he was never permitted to take up French nationality he lived all his life in France. He retained a fondness for England, and studied commerce in London for four years in the 1850s. However, his first love was painting, and his prosperous parents indulged their son and subsidized his studies at Gleyre's studio in 1862, where he met Renoir, Monet and Bazille. His parents were ruined by the Franco-Prussian war of 1870, and suddenly Sisley had to support himself by painting – and he was never again out of financial difficulties.

As a founder member of the group, he benefited greatly from working with Monet and the others, and from the interchange of ideas. There was a flowering of his art in the 1870s, to which the two examples here bear eloquent witness, but the museums are full of many rather ordinary and uninspired canvases. It has been suggested that when he was forced to paint for a living, he was unable consistently to maintain freshness and spontaneity at the high level set by, say, Monet.

He contributed to the first Impressionist exhibition and subsequently to three others. He painted on several brief occasions in England, but mostly confined himself to the environs of Paris. He preferred landscapes, and his style barely changed during the rest of his life; indeed he was apparently totally satisfied with Impressionism, unlike his colleagues, who all experimented with alternative styles and techniques. Sisley prophesied that his work would fail to be accepted until after he died, and he was proved right.

Canal Saint-Martin, Paris, 1870. Oil on canvas, 55 x 74cm. Oskar Reinhart Collection, Winterthur.

At about this time, Sisley's palette, which had tended to be rather sombre in the manner of the Barbizon group, lightened and became more Impressionist, largely as a result of working out of doors with Monet. His early influences probably also included Constable and Turner, whose work he would have seen in England as a student. This particular painting was actually accepted by the Salon of 1870; certainly the Impressionists did sometimes have works accepted by the Salon jury, even in those early days.

Floods at Port Marley, 1876. Oil on canvas, 60 x 81cm. Louvre, Paris.

This is only one of several versions he did of these floods, first in *1872,* and again in *1876* when another flood occurred. The Impressionists particularly delighted in large areas of water whose surfaces provided infinite potential for painting reflections. There is no sense of what must have been a tragedy – the scene might even be normal considering the lack of drama. Yet the turbulent black clouds do have a forboding aspect which cannot be ignored.

Here we have an example of Sisley's painting reaching peaks of greatness, which it sometimes did during this period of the *1870's,* even though he was undergoing severe personal hardship. His father's bankruptcy and death in *1870* left him without the support to which he was accustomed, and it was hard for him to earn a living from his painting.

In all Degas' ballet paintings, the main focus of attention is on the individual rather than the performance. Even where a performance is in progress, he could never resist drawing attention to a girl adjusting a shoe, or some similar human touch. The unconventional shape of this picture, and the similarity of the model, both in appearance and pose, suggest that this is a series of sketches of the same person from different angles, put together on the canvas in the form of a frieze.

Dancers Adjusting Their Slippers, *c.*1883. Oil on canvas, 70.5 x 101cm. The Cleveland Museum of Art, Gift of Hanna Fund.

EDGAR DEGAS 1834–1917

Degas is regarded as an Impressionist because of his close observation and depiction of genre scenes. He rarely painted landscapes or still lifes, or worked in the open air, and his career charted a more independent course than that of his associates.

His parents were wealthy and cultured, and he had relatives amongst the nobility – in fact his name was really De Gas (the prefix 'De' indicates nobility), and was later contracted to 'Degas'. He was not obliged to paint to live, but rather lived to paint. He was even encouraged in his ambition as a young man, his father being a lover of the arts, especially music and the theatre. Degas studied art seriously in Paris in 1852–54, and then went on regular trips to Italy, staying with relatives. He spent much time researching the old masters, both in Italy and in Paris. He also met one great master, Ingres, in 1855, who urged him to 'draw lines' – advice which he never forgot. His early works show considerable influence of Ingres, particularly in subject matter.

Degas was not a very sociable man, and he never married. He did meet Mary Cassatt when she came to Paris from America in about 1877, and they were mutual admirers of each others' work. But there is little evidence of intimacy – in fact, Mary Cassatt, like most of Degas' colleagues, found his pessimism and extreme political views very depressing. The man was a brilliant draughtsman, and this talent, combined with his unique and close observation of seemingly trivial details, gave his art exceptional quality. He frequently depicted dancers adjusting their ballet shoes or clothing, or indulging in a yawn or a stretch. His compositions were often unusual; the large open foregrounds, the singular angles and asymmetry, shocked some contemporary critics. These innovations were lifted by Degas from Japanese prints, then circulating amongst artists and connoisseurs, and also from the new art of photography. He deliberately avoided sentimental storytelling pictures, so beloved of the Victorians and so common at that time in West European painting.

His eyesight deteriorated seriously towards the end of his career, which in part caused him to turn to pastels, with their vivid colours, and with which he felt at home because of his love of drawing. Tragically the last ten years of his life were spent in fruitless frustration, since he went totally blind. His final works before he gave up all art in 1908 (he lived until 1917) were sculptures, since he could model by feeling with his hands.

Degas rarely painted the ballet performance; it was nearly always the rehearsal. There he could observe idiosyncratic touches of behaviour, such as the dancer adjusting her shoe, a seated girl scratching her back, another stretching and yawning. Beyond is the grace of the dancer on her points, under the direction of the unlikely-looking ballet master in his top hat, astride his chair (see detail). This is an early ballet composition, executed in a warm pinkish-grey monochrome. Degas obviously had to make some alterations, because one can see feet below the girls on the left and the seated girl's dress was once longer. His paint was applied too thinly to obscure these changes, perhaps because he intended to colour it later, but never finished it – there are not many monochrome paintings by Degas.

The Ballet Rehearsal, c.1873–74. Oil on canvas, 65 x 81cm. Louvre, Paris.

Degas

L'Absinthe *once belonged to a Scottish collector, and he showed it in London in 1893 under its original title* At the Café. *It aroused an outburst of self-righteous indignation, and was considered a picture of degradation and dissolution – not the sort of thing Art should perpetuate! (Everyone seemed to have forgotten Hogarth's* Rake's Progress *of a century earlier). In fact Degas, who shied away from the moralistic tale, intended it as no more than a pensive portrait of the actress Ellen Andrée and the Bohemian painter Desboutin, who is drinking nothing stronger than black coffee. They are seated at the Café de la*

Nouvelle-Athènes, which became the favourite meeting place of artists and writers after Desboutin decided the Café Guerbois was too rowdy! Desboutin was a very colourful character, who claimed noble ancestry and once lived in a vast castle in Italy, but lost his fortune. The composition is an example of one of Degas' favourite devices – placing the figures off centre with an expanse of largely unoccupied foreground.

L'Absinthe, 1876. Oil on canvas, 92 x 68cm. Louvre, Paris.

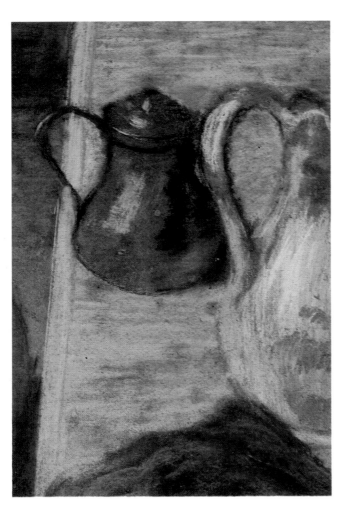

The Tub, 1886. Pastel, 60 x 83cm. Louvre, Paris.

Degas turned in his later years to pastel, a medium he enjoyed for its immediacy of colour, and also because of his facility in drawing. Perhaps because of his failing eyesight he needed these bright colours, although this particular example is very delicate in tone. It is amazing how many colours can be found in one single flesh area if inspected closely; yet from a distance the colours blend to suggest the lights and darks of the different contours. A brilliant touch is the light chalk stroke on the girl's left ear, enlivening an area otherwise submerged in deep shadow.

Many of these pastels are of women busy with their toilet, seen as if through a key-hole, viewed from behind and captured unawares. Degas had the models pose for him in his studio, amongst a collection of tubs and other props he had gathered for the purpose. They were generally awkward poses, but Degas never leaves ambiguities in the drawings.

The Tub includes a rare still life of the girl's toilet articles on the shelf behind her, and the detail shows how well he captures the metallic sheen of the little copper pot.

Still Life with Basket, *c.*1888–90. Oil on canvas, 65 x 85cm. Louvre, Paris.

Cézanne's still lifes were composed with the utmost care, as a contemporary has recorded who saw him arranging the objects for a painting. He often used the same props; for instance, the ginger jar in this painting frequently recurs. And he rarely painted a still life without the ubiquitous fruit – the soft round shapes of apples (a particular favourite because of their varying colours), oranges, peaches or pears. It is interesting to observe how the rounded contours of the fruit and the pottery are

Cézanne

PAUL CEZANNE 1839–1906

Cézanne was profoundly influenced early in his career by Pissarro. He helped Cézanne to lighten his palette and abandon the thick, heavy colours he had been using; he encouraged him to use primary colours, and to paint out of doors. Cézanne's work developed in such an individual way that he is usually not considered as a pure Impressionist, but rather as having gone one step further by providing the main link with Cubism, wherein lay the foundations of abstract art. But his adoption of many Impressionist techniques and his links with the movement justify his inclusion in this book.

There could not have been two more different artists than Cézanne and Degas. For the latter, line meant everything. Cézanne was not a natural draughtsman – technique came to him with difficulty at first. But once he had achieved facility in painting he obtained his results by constructing forms with planes of colour, almost in an architectural manner. He was concerned to convey the *inner* structure of the objects he painted, rather than just the surface appearance; and therein lies the real difference between Cézanne and the other Impressionists.

Despite his bourgeois upbringing – he was the son of a prosperous banker in the south of France – he rather revelled in uncouth behaviour, particularly towards the more refined members of the group such as Manet. His father had very reluctantly allowed him to follow the uncertain career of an artist, and although when he died in 1886 he left his son well provided for, he by no means consistently supported him. Cézanne's most serious financial difficulties occurred when his father ceased his support upon finding out about his son's long-standing liaison with Hortense Fiquet, who did not become his wife until 1886 – sixteen years after he first met her, and fourteen years after the birth of their son Paul.

Cézanne's financial independence meant that he could work consistently without the need to exhibit and sell, although he did paint regularly for his patron Victor Chocquet from 1875, the year Renoir introduced them. Consequently, when his paintings were shown at a big retrospective exhibition in 1895, they were a revelation to an astonished world, and particularly so to his fellow artists. This brought him belated fame, which Cézanne at first regarded with suspicion; later, however, he came to hope that his work would be continued by the next generation – as indeed it was. He worked intensively until the end, which came in October 1906, when he was overcome by a violent rain storm while out painting. He was brought home unconscious and died a few days later.

reflected in the handle of the basket and that of the ginger jar; and the whole is balanced by the firm horizontals and verticals of the furniture and floor. The number of colours he manages to incorporate into an object such as a white tablecloth is astonishing, yet one never doubts the validity of a single one.

The intense brilliance of the colours in this masterpiece are achieved despite the thin application of the paint – a far cry from the heavy impasto of his early work. It dates from a period of masterly activity, but nevertheless his paintings were continually rejected by the official Salon. The unfinished appearance of some of the objects seems a deliberate rebuff to those with a taste for smooth finished Salon works. The composition is rather reminiscent of Degas in its unorthodoxy – in particular the cutting in half of the brown bottle on the left. A chronology of Cézanne's work is practically impossible for works of this period, as he rarely dated anything.

Blue Vase, c.1885–87. Oil on canvas, 61 x 50cm. Louvre, Paris.

Cézanne, like Monet, painted some subjects many times over – but unlike Monet, his scenes were not the same view seen in different atmospheric conditions; he instead sought to convey the underlying structure of the objects. Mont Sainte-Victoire was a mountain near his native Aix-en-Provence, the country he loved so dearly and painted so frequently. There are Impressionistic elements here – small brushstrokes and light bright colours; but he includes the forbidden black, and blocks in the main shapes in wedges and planes, in a manner alien to his colleagues.

Mont Sainte-Victoire, 1885–87. Oil on canvas, 66 x 90cm. Courtauld Institute Galleries, London.

This is one of five versions of Card Players, *produced at Aix. The subject was suggested to Cézanne by a picture he saw in Aix museum of seventeenth-century peasant card players from the studio of the brothers Le Nain. As well as being a revealing study of two men in the act of concentration, it is also a study of shapes and planes, with rich colour contrasts, causing the picture to vibrate. These elements, combined with the slight left-wards tilt, give movement to an essentially static subject. The firmly vertical bottle in the centre of the table in the Louvre version here becomes a faint shadow, just discernible against the background with which it merges in an abstract pattern.*

The Card Players, *c.*1892. Oil on canvas, 60 x 72cm. Courtauld Institute Galleries, London.

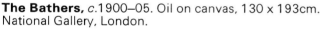

Probably the earliest of three large-scale paintings of bathers, this was nevertheless painted during Cézanne's last years. He was fascinated by the Renaissance theme of nude figures in a landscape, and frequently tackled it during his career, but until now only on a much smaller scale. The simplified angles and planes were to have an influence on the Cubists who saw it exhibited in Paris in 1907, the year after Cézanne's death.
In 1904, the painter Emile Bernard asked Cézanne why his nudes were so distorted. Cézanne replied that at his age he was shy to paint a young naked girl from life, and thought if he did so it might scandalize the neighbours, so he was using studies made in his student days.

The Bathers, c.1900–05. Oil on canvas, 130 x 193cm.
National Gallery, London.

Une Baignade, Asnières, 1883–84. Oil on canvas, 201 x 301 cm. National Gallery, London.

This composition dates from the period in which Seurat was already developing his pointillist *technique, though he had not yet adopted it. There is still an Impressionist feel about the painting, though the solid forms and firm outlines of the figures remind one of Renoir during his 'dry' period. It is an enormous painting, and the careful composition is most impressive with the monumental and motionless groups being reminiscent of the great fifteenth century Italian painter, Piero della Francesca. In 1884 Seurat and Odilon Redon participated in the founding of a* Société des Indépendants, *and Une Baignade was exhibited in the first salon of this group. In 1886 it went to New*

GEORGES SEURAT 1859–1891

Seurat's system of painting is termed *pointillism* after the myriad little dots or points with which he covered his canvases. His ideas were based on the colour and optical theories of certain contemporary scientists, in particular Chevreul, whom he visited in 1884. However, Seurat passionately disputed suggestions that he had not himself originated this 'method', as he called it. The tiny dots are juxtaposed in such a way that from a distance they appear to blend and form a solid colour; but if viewed very close, you see a mass of multi-coloured dots – somewhat similar to what you would see if you looked at colour offset printing through a strong magnifier

He interested several other artists in his method, notably Pissarro and Signac, and they formed themselves into a group of 'Neo-Impressionists'. This was more a deliberate reaction against Impressionism than an extension of their ideas. The method included scientific analysis and painstaking execution according to strict principles, whereas the true Impressionists recorded the effects of atmosphere, movement and light on their canvases with quick, short brushstrokes. Nevertheless, Seurat exhibited **La Grande Jatte** (pages -55) at the eighth Impressionist exhibition in 1886 at the invitation of Pissarro, but not without opposition from some of the other artists, and severe rebuffs from the critics.

Seurat lost the support of Pissarro, who became dissatisfied with Neo-Impressionism in 1889 and returned to his old style. Consequently the group broke up. Only two years later, Seurat, who remained trenchantly faithful to his method, fell ill and died within a few days – at the age of only 32.

York for Durand-Ruel's exhibition of Impressionists of Paris, *but it won little approval, although it attracted much notice at both shows. The location is a bathing spot at Asnières on the Seine ('une baignade' means 'a bathing place').*

A Sunday Afternoon at La Grande-Jatte, 1884–86.
Oil on canvas, 206.3 x 308.6cm. Art Institute of Chicago.

Seurat

As with Une Baignade, *this canvas was composed from a series of small sketches made on the spot and then painted in the studio. It was Seurat's first major work to be completed in his purely* pointillist *style, and the climax of his lengthy researches into optical and colour theory.*

The scene is a wonderful record of middle class suburban life in the 1880's, but the technique is so riveting that it almost excludes all else. The frieze-like appearance is achieved by the frozen immobility of everything and everyone, even though people and dogs are portrayed as walking and running and engaged in a number of activities. It is a picture full of extraordinary contradictions – yet it is a masterpiece.

VINCENT VAN GOGH 1853–1890

Van Gogh's career as a practising artist was extremely short – from 1882 to 1890 when he died, although he did show artistic talent in his youth and worked for a time in the fine art trade.

He was born in 1853, the son of a Dutch clergyman whose family had connections with the art dealer Goupil. Vincent was employed at Goupil's for a time, first in Paris and then in London, where he encountered his first disappointment in love. Because of his fiery temperament, he often became involved in situations he could not handle, such as his deep, unrequited love for his landlady's daughter. Her rejection of him made him bitter and introverted. Over the following five years he attempted to achieve acceptable status as an evangelist, and his passionate and critical views alienated his family and friends, who in vain tried to help him. During a period spent preaching amongst the Belgian mining community with whom he deliberately shared squalor and deprivation, he perceived his true vocation to be a painter. In the years 1882–86 he underwent intensive training in The Hague and Antwerp, and then went to stay in Paris with his younger brother Theo, who also worked at Goupil's.

The most famous work of his pre-Parisian period is **The Potato Eaters**, a group of poor Brabant peasants, with whom he felt great sympathy following his experiences in the mining community. Van Gogh is often considered the first *Ex*pressionists, because he allowed his feelings and emotions to be expressed on the canvas in a forceful and effective way.

During a two-year stay in Paris in 1886–8, van Gogh became excited by the Impressionists and assimilated many of their ideas. He saw their works at exhibitions, and met Pissarro, who taught him the Impressionists' colour and light theories as well as Seurat's *pointillist* method. Van Gogh's palette consequently lightened, and he used smaller brushstrokes. He also came into contact with the Symbolists and much admired Puvis de Chavannes; but he never became wedded to the Symbolist ideal as Gaugin did.

Another major influence encountered in Paris was the Japanese print. After his removal to Arles in 1888 he felt almost as if he were in (what he imagined to be) Japan. Many of his paintings show the strong influence of these prints, including **Peach Tree in Bloom**.

From Arles he wrote regularly to his brother Theo, bequeathing to us a full and touching account of his daily activities and thoughts on art. His painting at this time is full of expression and vigour, completely assured in its handling. Gaugin visited him in the winter of 1888. This proved disastrous for both of them, as these two opposite personalities clashed irrevocably, culminating in Vincent's desperate gesture of despair in cutting off part of his ear. He went to the mental hospital at Saint Rémy in 1889, where he continued to paint, but the following year, feeling compelled to return north, he stayed in the care of Dr. Gachet in Auvers-sur-Oise. His work there became erratic and traumatic, and his paintings of cornfields express his loneliness and desolation. The famous **Crows in a Cornfield** with its lowering sky, enormous birds and the three divergent paths, was completed only a few days before he shot himself.

Peach Tree in Bloom, 1888. Oil on canvas, 81 x 60cm. National Museum Vincent van Gogh, Amsterdam.

The influence of the Japanese print is clearly seen in the simple flat design of this painting. Van Gogh collected these prints during his first visit to Paris in 1886. They were widely circulated and were influential on many of van Gogh's contemporaries, especially the Impressionists. There is another version of this picture, painted in memory of Mauve, his former teacher in The Hague, who had recently died. Van Gogh sent it from Arles as a gift to the family.

Painted in the autumn of 1888, just before Gaugin joined him, this work suggests that van Gogh was already entering a period of depression. His letters to Theo inform us that he wanted 'to express the idea that the café is a place where one can ruin oneself, go mad or commit a crime'. This was actually written about the companion to this picture which shows the interior, but the enticing night lights of the café in contrast to the dark night are no less suggestive. He proclaimed his enormous interest in 'the problem of painting night scenes and effects on the spot' in a letter about this work. That interest he pursued, culminating in the despairing Starry Night painted during his stay in the Saint Rémy asylum.*

Outdoor Café, 1888. Oil on canvas, 81 x 65.5cm. Kröller-Müller Stichting, Otterlo. Left, detail from **Outdoor Café**.

Fields of corn always meant a great deal to van Gogh. Sowing signified the creation of life, and the harvest, the cutting of the corn, symbolised death. The yellow colour (surely his favourite) expressed 'health and the source of strength'. The significance of these feelings was most expressively demonstrated at the end of his life in the picture Crows in a Cornfield, *an intense and desperately emotional painting by a man unstable in mind.* The Harvest *in comparison is a serene, peaceful Provencal scene near Arles where he lived in 1888.*

The Harvest, 1888. Oil on canvas, 73 x 92cm. National Museum Vincent van Gogh, Amsterdam.

PAUL GAUGUIN 1848–1903

Legendary, scandalous, disastrous – these adjectives have frequently been used to describe Paul Gauguin's life, and indeed they are far from inaccurate. Yet amidst this disarray, his great genius was eventually acclaimed as one of the most startling developments to emerge from Impressionism. Certainly his artistic roots are buried in Impressionism. When he took up painting, first as a Sunday painter and later full time, he studied with Pissarro – the conscientious instructor of the young and talented in the next generation. Gauguin first saw Pissarro's paintings in the house of his guardian, who had a fine picture collection and who encouraged Gauguin in his new enthusiasm for art. Although it is from this time that the storms in his life really blew up, nevertheless his youth and origins were not without unusual incident.

His maternal grandmother had been a revolutionary in the early part of the century, with aristocratic Peruvian connections. The first seven years of Gauguin's life were spent in Peru, in exotic and tropical surroundings which haunted him all his days. In his late teens he served in the French navy, travelling the world, and later on the prospect of long sea journeys never daunted him. Upon his marriage in 1873 to a young Danish governess, Mette, he at first settled down to a straightforward, bourgeois existence under the paternal eye of the guardian neighbour who had promised his dying mother to look after him. He had five children and became quite a successful and affluent stockbroker. But the awakened interest in art gradually possessed

his thought, and a stock-market crash in 1882 provided the opportunity for him to make the break. His wife was never able to adapt to the dramatic change in fortune and way of life, and thereafter the marriage deteriorated. Mette returned to Denmark with the children and Gauguin remained a penniless artist for the rest of his life.

The first phase of his art was Impressionist, influenced by Pissarro and Cézanne. The next phase evolved at Pont Aven in Brittany, where a circle of artists gathered about him. Here he gradually 'synthesised' (as he put it) his own ideas, the ideas of Impressionism and other artistic currents, such as Symbolism. His colours became bright and solid, applied in broad, flat planes, with black outlines; and the subject matter became deeply symbolic.

One interesting but typically traumatic experience took place at Arles in 1888, where he went at the invitation of Vincent van Gogh in order to paint with him and form the nucleus of an artistic brotherhood. Their opposite temperaments and talents clashed disastrously, and the gory climax at the end of two months arrived when Vincent cut off part of his own ear as a hideous gesture of protest at their incompatibility. Gauguin fled and Vincent ended up in an asylum.

This, together with various other humiliating experiences he suffered, turned Gauguin's gaze towards the tropics, which beckoned him compellingly. He left for Tahiti in 1891, anticipating a life of native simplicity with no need for money (which he did not have) and a ready supply of half naked models. He found the latter, but was frustrated by

various colonial customs and the constant lack of funds. Nevertheless, from 1891 to 1903 when he died (aged fifty five) he produced a succession of brilliant canvases of tropical scenes and golden bodies – the greatest and best-known phase of his art. He spent the rest of his life on these islands, with the exception of a two-year interlude in France.

He did not escape difficulties and obstacles as he had hoped; some, indeed, such as legal and financial wrangles, were self-inflicted because of his fiery temperament; and he was wracked with devastating sickness. Yet the masterpieces flowed from his brush, unique, unlike anything the world had seen. Only at the end did they begin to become accepted, and that partly because his prolonged absence provided a romantic legend that stimulated interest. And of course after he died the prices immediately soared.

Gauguin painted this as his final testament before attempting suicide. He had returned in 1895 to Tahiti after an abortive two-year visit to France. His affairs hardly improved, but rather grew worse. He had no money and was desperately ill with syphillis which eventually killed him. Following a series of disasters, he suffered a succession of heart attacks. He wrote, 'I can see no way out, except Death which brings absolute deliverance.' He had painted nothing for many months, but now embarked on his most ambitious picture, and painting like one possessed produced this masterpiece. He left a detailed description of it, which aids our interpretation. The picture should be read from right to left, in the oriental manner. It starts with birth – with the sleeping baby, and ends on the left with the old woman near death. The central figure is of a man picking fruit, which symbolises the pleasures of life, harvest and fertility. The idol in the background of the left-hand section menaces this ideal of happiness. To Gauguin, the whole thing was a dream, a recapturing of his childhood Eden, but with the dark side of life lurking as an ominous threat, constantly there in the background.

His suicide attempt failed. The arsenic he took in such a massive dose only made him very sick. He lived on for another five years and painted some more superb pictures, but the period of his greatest artistic activity was over.

Where Do We Come From, What Are We, Where Are We Going? 1897. Oil on canvas, 139 x 375cm. Museum of Fine Arts, Boston.

When Will You Marry? 1892. Oil on canvas, 105 x 77.5cm. Rodolphe Staechelin Collection, Basle.

Painted the year after Gauguin first arrived in Tahiti, the picture is exuberant with brilliance and colour, reflecting Gauguin's contentment (albeit shortlived) at this time. After his initial arrival in Tahiti and the shock of finding the capital Papeete so expensive – not the primitive place he anticipated – he moved to the other end of the island and lived in a hut on the beach amongst the natives. He took a 'wife' – a thirteen year old girl called Tehura, whom he described in his auto-biographical book Noa Noa *at some length. He painted many pictures of her, and although it would be pure speculation to suggest that she provided the inspiration for this, it is not unlikely in view of the title.*

Riding was the most practical means of transportation in the Pacific islands when Gauguin lived there. He included horses in several of his canvases, but in this there is an overtone of symbolism.

His paintings prior to his return to France in September *1893* were mostly narratives depicting the daily lives of the natives, particularly the women. After his return to Tahiti in *1895*, many of the pictures were laden with heavy symbolism. This is one of the most elusive of Gauguin's works in the second Tahitian period, for we know so little of its meaning. But he did say that he intended the 'luxuriant nature' to convey the mystery of Tahiti.

Prior to its coming to the Louvre, the painting was owned by Daniel de Monfreid, the one trusted friend Gauguin had all the years he was in the South Seas, and who was largely responsible for Gauguin's eventual but posthumous acceptance.

The White Horse, 1898. Oil on canvas, 141 x 91cm. Louvre, Paris.

ACKNOWLEDGEMENTS

Colour transparencies have been
kindly loaned by the following:
Stedelijk Museum, Amsterdam
Arts Graphiques de la Cité, Paris
Blauel, Munich
Boston Museum of Fine Arts
Art Institute of Chicago
Cleveland Museum of Art
Courtauld Institute Galleries, London
Giraudon, Paris
Hans Hinz
Kultura, Budapest
Los Angeles County Museum of Art
National Gallery, London
Metropolitan Museum of Art, New York
Kröller-Müller Stichting, Otterlo
Scala, Florence
National Gallery of Art, Washington
Phillips Collection, Washington
Oskar Reinhart Collection, Winterthur